Readers and
in the
Church of England

Carolyn Headley

Tutor in Liturgy and Spirituality, Wycliffe Hall, Oxford

GROVE BOOKS LIMITED
RIDLEY HALL RD CAMBRIDGE CB3 9HU

Contents

Acknowledgements

I am indebted to a number of Readers and others who have contributed to the updating of this booklet. In particular I wish to thank Pat Nappin (Honorary Secretary Central Readers Council), Wendy Thorpe (National Moderator of Reader Training), Anna de Lange, Malcolm Lambert, Paul Baguley, John King, and the Group for Renewal of Worship.

The Cover Illustration is by Tamsin Merchant

First Impression January 1991
Reprinted January 1994
Second Edition January 2001
ISSN 0144-1728
ISBN 1 85174 463 0

1
Introduction

When the first edition of the Grove booklet *Readers and Worship in the Church of England* was written in 1991 we were celebrating 125 years since the revival of the modern office of Reader. The great gathering at the NEC in Birmingham testified to the strength and dynamism of Reader ministry, at a time when it stood at the forefront of the debate on how local ministry should be recognized. There was a growing diversification in recognition of both lay and ordained ministry that continued to develop throughout the 1990s. So now there is a great variety of ways in which dioceses and individual parishes authorize and enable those who wish to serve God. A Reader may minister alongside other licensed lay ministers and those with diocesan recognition of specific areas of ministry, Ordained Local Ministers, and Non-Stipendiary Deacons and Priests, as well as those in the more traditional clergy roles, and those without any formal authorization who are given opportunity to exercise their God-given gifts.[1] Within this array of ministers Readers number approximately 10,000—as many as the ordained stipendiary clergy. They are a significant and important part of the Church's ministry.

A number of reports and documents over recent years have provided guidelines for good practice, drawn attention to the issues Readers face, and encouraged Reader ministry. The Central Readers' Council has developed and been instrumental in many good things happening, including the re-launch of a lively and informative format for *The Reader* magazine. Many of the hopes for Reader ministry in the early 1990s are now common expectations, but not all.

This booklet aims to provide information about the current role of Readers, particularly related to worship; to point to some of the opportunities and challenges that Readers face; to provide an introduction to Reader ministry for those who are investigating a calling to it; to serve as a handbook for licensed Readers; to underline the responsibilities that we all share in fostering Reader ministry and using it well; and to give a handy summary of ideas and information that can be found elsewhere, but are not necessarily readily to hand.

This is essentially an updated version of the booklet written in 1991, so a few sections will be unaltered. However, it is also different in many places. Those who have used the first booklet have fed in ideas for its improvement, and a number of Readers, from different parts of the country and engaged in different spheres of ministry, have contributed to this present text.

---

1   See *Stranger in the Wings*, A Report on Non-Stipendiary Ministry (ABM Policy paper No 8, 1998).

2

The Nature of Reader Ministry

The Reader's Calling

The visible role of a Reader on a Sunday morning may appear to be very similar to that of others who minister. In function there may be little to distinguish them. A number of both ordained and lay licensed workers have similar restrictions in liturgy to those of a Reader. Many of these are similarly non-stipendiary, operating at a comparable level of time commitment. There is also a groundswell of confidence in 'the priesthood of all believers' which encourages all church members to use their gifts, and for some this will include leading worship and preaching. These developments enrich the life of the church, but blur the edges of distinction between ministries.

This is a good and positive development in the life of the church. However, it can then be argued that there is no need for someone to do a three-year training, be admitted to an office, and be licensed in order to minister. So Readers can wonder why they have done all this when anyone else can be asked to do the same things at the services—even though regulations require a bishop's licence for preaching and his permission for distributing Communion.

The practice of being set apart and specifically commissioned to lead God's people is founded on biblical principles. A trained, able, recognized ministry acts as a focus for the calling of each member of the church. This essentially is the meaning of ordination itself. Over recent years the greater flexibility in the ordained ministry has meant that many people have full-time secular jobs whilst being ordained. It can therefore be argued that if their ministry is acceptable to the wider church, and the functions are similar, that Readers are in practice exercising at least a diaconal role, and should be ordained.

So what is distinctive about a Reader's calling, when they could have the same *function* if they were either unlicensed lay persons or were to be ordained in a way which valued their secular role as well as their ministry within the parish?

The specific role of Readers is defined not so much by their function, as by their identity as theologically trained lay people whose ministry is recognized not only locally but by the wider church. In a church where ordination has tended to emphasize the separate nature of ordained clergy, Readers can more easily be the focus of the lay ministry, which needs to be part of the daily life of the church. The liturgical role of a trained, licensed, lay person speaks of the value of all the laity and recognizes the distinctive contribution and the worth of their ministry. It is a complementary ministry bringing the *laos* into the focal point of church life—the worship. Not only does it act as a focus, but also as a role-model, or flagship.

Greater participation of the laity in the liturgy gives the visible message that it is the whole church family that is worshipping together. It speaks of God's desire to work in and through each one of us, and of the presence of his Holy Spirit in all believers. It ensures that those who are known to have gifts and abilities, which will help build up the church in worship and faith, are not denied their ministry. It brings complementary gifts and experience of life and the world to the ministry team. The Reader's calling is not only to be a focus for all lay ministry, but also to positively enable, nurture and encourage the calling of all laity to use the gifts that God gives to his body, the church. It therefore follows that Readers should be careful not to block out or undervalue other lay ministry by being possessive in ministry terms.

The question of whether Readers should be ordained is being asked again by some at this time, and further reports are expected concerning the place and role of the diaconate, which may affect how Reader ministry is perceived. However, a proposal to ordain Readers undermines their distinctive calling. Their very lay-ness is their strength and their offering to the ministry of the church. For some Readers ordination to the permanent diaconate may be appropriate as fulfilment of their personal calling, but it would be detrimental to signify that ordination was necessary for any Reader's ministry. Now that Deaconesses are a declining order and fewer people are called to be Parish Workers, Readers are the principal canonically recognized lay order. The discussion over the nature of ordination, and the theology of the three-fold orders of the church, needs to take into account the value of all lay ministry, and the place of those prepared to undergo significant training and theological study as a basis for ministry without being ordained.

If the positive and distinctive role of Readers is accepted then this may overcome some of the prejudices and shortcomings of the past. Some clergy may need to examine the attitudes they have towards Readers, and opportunities they offer. Sometimes experience has given a limited picture of Reader ministry, or there has been disappointment in what a Reader has done, making some incumbents wary of Reader ministry. Readers need to be careful over the standard of the ministry they offer, and be willing to be adaptable and adventurous. They also need to have confidence in their calling—not wishing they were the vicar, or holding on to secret desires to be ordained, but rejoicing in the contribution that they can make as valued members of the church's ministry.

The congregations need to recognize the bridging role of the Reader in valuing both their 'up-front' ministry and their identity with the congregation as fellow lay people. If licensing is seen as the Reader becoming 'one of them' instead of 'one of us,' then much of the value of subsequent ministry is lost before it begins. The congregation should see Readership as a sign that all lay ministry is affirmed, and be encouraged by it, valuing the complementary role of different forms of ministry. Where Reader ministry is new to a parish it will be necessary to teach a congregation about the role of a Reader, in order to maximize the potential and avoid misunderstandings or false expectations.

The fact that Readers are admitted to a canonical office, and receive a licence to minister, inevitably and purposefully gives them authority. The authority needs to arise in the first place from that given by God, evidenced by gifts which are recognized by the congregation and incumbent, showing that a person is being called and equipped by God to minister. The selection process of the wider church affirms the call, and the training develops the God-given gifts. Finally the Reader is licensed, which marks the beginning of a publicly recognized ministry.[2]

The public licensing is therefore the completion of a process that begins long before. A service in the church where the Reader will minister, conducted by the bishop or his representative, will clearly state the relationship to the parish, the incumbent, and the people. If the licensing takes place centrally in the diocese, or at a small meeting or privately, then some subsequent public act in the local church (or place of ministry) would be of great value to Reader and congregation alike. Support from fellow Readers and local clergy is also to be encouraged at the licensing.

Great care needs to be taken in discerning the call to minister. If a Reader has to stand on the authority of robes and a licence, and sees these as defending a right to a position of power and status, then something has gone very wrong in the early stages of testing that call. Sadly there are instances of this with which the church has to live (as with some ordained clergy), but these are exceptions rather than the rule.

The Ministry of Readers

Readers exercise a wide range of ministries. The recent papers on selection,[3] Reader ministry and training,[4] and Bishops' regulations for Reader ministry,[5] all give a clear picture of a ministry which is primarily preaching, teaching and worship leading, but is also likely to include pastoral and educational work, evangelism and other forms of lay leadership. Consequently their authorization encompasses a wide range of possible duties, and their selection and training should enable all aspects of ministry to develop.

The individual gifts of Readers will in part determine the scope of their ministry in a particular situation. Most Readers are parish-based with a preaching, teaching and service-leading ministry. Readers are licensed to preach at any of the services, whether Communion or not (which has been so since 1969), but their contribution relating to ministry of the Word need not be limited to the preaching slot. Communication of the faith can take place in a variety of situations, which will include teaching large groups, but will also include small groups, in home groups, and in the catechetical role of baptism preparation, confirmation classes, and *Alpha* and *Emmaus* groups etc. However, many also do pastoral visiting, distribute Holy Communion to the sick or in residential homes, and are involved in ministry to younger church members in children's Sunday groups and youth work. Some Readers are involved in counselling or spiritual direction. Some engagement with the pastoral work of a parish enables a Reader to gain a fuller

---

2   See *Bishops' Regulations for Reader Ministry*, Archbishops' Council (January 2000) p 5 re: Canon E6 and pp 12–13 re: Admission and Licensing.
3   ABM Policy Paper No 7, *Selection for Reader Ministry* (January 1998).
4   GS Misc 618, *Reader Ministry and Training, 2000 and Beyond*, Ministry Division (September 2000).
5   *Bishops' Regulations for Reader Ministry*, The Archbishops' Council (Church House, January 2000).

picture of the life and issues into which they need to speak in the preaching and teaching.

A few Readers are involved in sector ministry being prison, hospital or town centre chaplains, or chaplains to the forces, or to subsidiary organizations such as cadets or clubs for retired forces personnel. Some are involved in missionary work or are engaged by Christian organizations. The range of ministry is vast as recent editions of *The Reader* magazine demonstrate.[6] Even where not formally defined, Readers in rural situations and multi-benefice parishes will often be given responsibility for a particular community, or sphere of ministry in which they specialize. Most Readers are non-stipendiary although a few are employed for some of the sector ministries mentioned and there are now isolated instances of churches or parishes with a Reader-in-Charge.[7]

Whilst this booklet is primarily concerned with their role in preaching and worship leading, it must not be forgotten that the strength of Reader ministry lies in their involvement in the secular sphere as much as the local church. For some this is their prime place of ministry, being a witness to people in their local or working situation, or actively engaged in political, social and community projects.

As Readership is an office recognized by Canon, it carries with it the authority of the church, through the bishop. The legal parameters recognize and authorize the diversity of ministry that has developed over recent years. Appendix 1 quotes Canon E4, which outlines the potential areas of ministry. The breadth of permitted use is one reason why efforts to identify Readers by what they do rather than by what they are is unhelpful.

There are some areas of difficulty for Readers in the current profusion of forms of recognition of ministries, giving rise to tension in some situations. In some dioceses a vast number of lay ministries are individually recognized and bishop's authorization is given for exercising them within the area. This can include preaching, worship leading, distributing Communion in church and at home, pastoral visiting, healing ministry, youth ministry, administrative ministry, and many others. Some dioceses licence 'Commissioned Lay Ministers,' 'Pastoral Assistants,' and 'Lay Evangelists.' If Readers define themselves by the function of their ministry they can feel threatened by such diverse authorization, as a number of these areas of ministry would be seen as the function of a Reader. However, with a different view of Readership, as the principal canonically recognized lay ministry, it can be seen as the appropriate office to which widely gifted men and women are licensed, and that those with a more distinct but limited sphere of ministry are better authorized with more specific episcopal permission. Rather than feeling squeezed out by the richness of the ministry offered, Readers can then see their distinctive role as an important part of what God is doing in his church at this time. They can also be seen as lay leaders who are able to share in the teaching, facilitating and developing of the ministry of others.

---

6   See, for example, *The Reader*, Summer 2000, Volume 97, No 2.
7   *The Reader*, Autumn 2000, Volume 97 No 3, p 7: describes a stipendiary Reader-in-Charge of a rural united benefice.

Such a diverse ministry has led to some dissatisfaction with the name 'Reader,' for the duties that a Reader now performs go far beyond reading the service and a basic homily. As long ago as 1904 a monthly magazine called *The Reader and Lay Worker* (forerunner of *The Reader*) had a contribution from Dr Yeatman-Briggs (then suffragan Bishop of Suffolk) who wrote 'deprecating the title of "Reader" as not really expressing their work—an opinion shared by many others.'[8] Because of such dissatisfaction some dioceses have begun using different terms for Readers locally. The debate over this is likely to continue, although in many ways it is an insubstantial matter. Whatever its name, the ministry of Readership is developing as a very useful part of the wider ministry of the church.

Collaborative and Team Ministry

The emerging understanding of collaborative and team ministry is affirming lay leaders, Readers among them, and positively encouraging an understanding of their vital role. In areas where benefices have become larger and resources have become more stretched, their value is readily acknowledged. They contribute an enormous amount with commitment and self-sacrifice, without remuneration, and are often the principal minister in a community.

The ABM paper on *The Deployment of Readers* devotes a whole section to good practice related to the use of Readers in team and group ministries.[9] The situation is quite complex, with a variety of patterns existing throughout the country. There is also an element of experimentation taking place as the church tries to find good and appropriate ways of using limited resources. As the paper says 'All people in authorized ministry must work collaboratively and with generous give-and-take as they cater for the needs of other people.' Many Readers are being asked to be very flexible in their approach to ministry, with some being asked to minister in places of need away from their home church and others being asked to concentrate on one church community. See the section on Deployment for further discussion of this matter.

Having been trained and recognized by the wider church, the Reader has a place within the leadership of the local church. When the structure is traditional, with incumbent, churchwardens, standing committee, and perhaps an assistant curate or several ministers in a team ministry or multi-benefice situation, then a Reader should be seen to join that team on licensing. This includes invitation to staff meetings on a regular basis, involvement in long-term planning and goal-setting, and sharing in the leading and enabling of the congregation. This may mean having meetings at times of day when *all* the staff can be together, including those involved in secular employment. Readers are not automatically *ex officio* on the PCC; they may stand for election along with others, or be co-opted by the PCC. If not on the PCC then Readers will need to be included in other ways in

---

8   W S Williams, *A History of the Reader Movement in the Church of England* (Parrott and Neves Ltd (CRB), 1932).

9   ABM Ministry Paper No 20 *The Deployment of Readers: A way Forward in Ministry* (November 1998) pp 7–9, ¶ 26-33.

the consultation process of decision making, as part of the staff team. Invitation to clergy chapter meetings is also appreciated, at least on an occasional basis.

The situation is more complex in churches with larger lay ministry teams. Where there is an eldership or pastorate team, or where those with identifiable gifts of leading worship and preaching are encouraged to minister, here the Reader's role can become very squeezed. It is important that the relationship with other lay ministers is clear, and acceptable to all involved. 'Job descriptions' can sometimes help, or delegation of clear areas of responsibility, if arrived at through satisfactory discussion and negotiation and reviewed regularly.

The role given in worship needs to reflect the relationship, otherwise confusion and hurt arises. These in turn can lead to a Reader seeking status rather than fulfilment in ministry. Seeing the Reader leading worship, preaching, and praying supports and underlines the whole of their ministry.

The sharing of the liturgical role is not always easy for the incumbent. It involves trust, and giving over to someone else a very precious and important part of one's own ministry. It is sometimes therefore jealously guarded. Understandable though this may be there is so much to be gained from the wealth of experience and knowledge, gifts and insights, that can come from others. In worship the issues related to collaborative ministry are highlighted at the very core of the church's life. Simple decisions about the way worship is conducted, and what part various people are playing, will be affected by the way the deeper questions are handled. This may also involve those who are not gifted presiding over those who are gifted, whether that be Readers presiding over other lay people involved in an act of worship, or the incumbent presiding as a Reader ministers.

The concept of the president's role is at the heart of this area of debate. It is therefore only to be expected that there is a vast variety of practice. Some incumbents willingly share the leading of worship, and do not feel that the presidency is threatened (or do not have a strong concept of presidency anyway). For others this is a very difficult area to face, for, once their presidency is shared, they may well feel that there is a change to their very identity.

An appreciation of the positive contribution of a theologically trained lay minister should affect the way Readers are used. They should be asked to minister out of choice, as complementary to the ordained ministry, and alongside it, not as those whose only role is a pseudo-clerical gap-filling ministry. It is to be regretted that they have often been used just to give the vicar a night off, or just asked to minister at ailing and almost abandoned services, or used only if no one else can be found to give cover for an ordained clergyperson.

Collaborative ministry, which recognizes a variety of gifts and the ministry of all believers, can readily embrace Reader ministry as one expression of what God is doing through all the members of Christ's body in his church.

3
Readers in Liturgy

As already seen there is plenty of scope for Readers in ministry. The factors which affect their role therefore are more to do with their individual gifting, the local situation and diocesan policy, than with the legal limitations. In some areas these factors are limiting, and in others they are enabling. This section describes common practice and points to areas where the boundaries of Reader ministry have been pushed forward. In some dioceses as many as a quarter to a half of all services on a given Sunday will be led by Readers.

Ministers of the Word
i) Preaching from a Distinctive Worldview
The perspective, or worldview, that arises from secular involvement benefits the Reader's ministry. Those who are, or have recently been, employed in secular jobs will have a distinctive contribution to offer. This is not to say that full-time clergy are in some way 'out of this world' (!) or out of touch, but having someone in the ministry team whose sphere of daily work and life revolves around the secular thought patterns, vocabulary, values, and contacts of a non-church environment makes a valuable offering. Readers bring into a team the wisdom gained from living out the Christian life in the world. Being trained and informed they then apply theological reflection to what they experience, and can therefore bring fresh insights into the church's ministry.

Preaching is a prime function of the Reader as a communicator of the faith and minister of the Word. The emphasis in current training is on encouraging freedom and courage to preach from the heart out of their experience of life, with theological reflection. The methodology has changed from the essay-bound written expression of faith and theology to the more dynamic communication of projects, group work and presentations. It is hoped that with this will come a greater ability to communicate the faith naturally, greater flexibility in the types of events and venues in which Readers minister (from small informal house groups to large formal events and even rallies) and more discernment about which role-models to adopt in developing preaching style. (To 'clone' the vicar is not always the best way of communicating!)

ii) Planning the Preaching
Discussion over the direction of preaching and teaching for the parish would benefit from Reader input, whether this is in how to use the set lectionary readings as a programme of input, or in the working out of a preaching series. When a series is planned it is helpful to have group discussion with all those taking part to pool ideas, avoid duplication in the sermons, and stimulate greater depth of thinking. This is particularly important with the *Common Worship* lectionary.

One clear advantage of the *Common Worship* lectionary is an end to the allocation of readings according to the type of service. This produced a lot of problems for churches where there was a mix of Communion and other services. Now churches are able to follow one set of readings for the Principal, Second or Third services. The *Common Worship* lectionary has a principle of having semi-continuous reading of Scripture, which means that preaching will have a more systematic feel to it. However, within the provision it is necessary to choose whether the Old or New Testament readings are the basis for preaching, and at certain times of year different Tracks can also be followed. Co-ordination over the preaching has therefore become far more important than with the thematic approach of the ASB.

If not present when others are preaching, it is important for a Reader to find out exactly what approach has been followed in a church, which readings are the focus of the preaching, and whether the preaching should pick up a particular Track or series. This is likely to be necessary for Readers ministering in teams or groups, and those acting as visiting preachers. In the seasons where there is more freedom and the church can choose to depart from the lectionary readings, then particular care needs to be taken in planning the preaching. Sometimes sermons are taped and where this happens it is helpful to listen to the previous week's message in order to build on it and provide continuity in the exposition of Scripture or in the series being followed.

iii) Inviting Readers to Preach

Many Readers are underused by the church and could preach more often. Where there is a concentration of available Readers, then this potential could be used by parishes where the resources are more stretched. See the section on Deployment below.

Leading Non-Communion Services
i) A Service of the Word and Morning and Evening Prayer

These services are often taken by Readers officiating alone. In rural areas with multi-benefice situations the Reader may well become the minister to whom the community relates as 'vicar,' because the regular weekly service is not Communion. This is also the case for Readers in the forces, where chaplains sometimes cover several bases and can only visit occasionally. This being so, it is an important area of ministry, and one which brings Readers much fulfilment.

This is an area where Readers can have significant input into the development of the worship. Being able to identify with the congregation, but being aware of developments in the wider church, they can encourage change and growth. This is especially helpful in this time of liturgical development within the Church of England. The ASB has been superseded by *Common Worship* (from 3 December 2000), except in churches where episcopal permission is given for temporary extension to ASB use. The flexibility and potential of *Common Worship* liturgy means that those who use it need to be aware of liturgical principles and good practice related to worship. Readers are in a good position to lead local congregations in their understanding and use of the new services. They may also be involved in teaching related to the changes.[10]

The structure and guidelines of *A Service of the Word* can be used for any non-eucharistic service, or as the first part of a Holy Communion service. But as well as the basic outline, the main volume of *Common Worship* also contains Orders for Morning and Evening Prayer on Sunday. These are worked out examples of a how *A Service of the Word* can be used on a Sunday. Most sections of these services allow for variation in content, providing enormous potential for use of alternative resource material. Creativity and careful preparation is encouraged in the way any *Service of the Word* is led and its individual parts presented.

Many Readers will also be asked to lead occasional services for special occasions. When not used as the principal service of the day, the scope for flexibility in using *A Service of the Word* is even greater. Family or All Age Services, ecumenical services, services of celebration or linked to local events, outreach or mission services, and seasonal acts of worship, such as meditations and acts of devotion in Advent or Lent or Holy Week, can all use *A Service of the Word* as a basis. Readers will often be involved in this ministry, and need to be able to make good use of such flexibility, and to be courageous in leading worship that will minister to those they serve.

However, they will also find that it is the *Book of Common Prayer* that is still required in many places, and decisions about how much innovation is appropriate will need to be made according to knowledge of the congregation. For example the main volume of *Common Worship* contains the BCP services of Morning and Evening Prayer with some shortening and simplification, reflecting common practice in many churches. The provision enabling these services to be produced is entitled *The Schedule of Permitted Variations to The Book Of Common Prayer Orders for Morning and Evening Prayer where these occur in Common Worship*.[11] Using these services from small off-print editions of *Common Worship*, or produced onto card for local use, may be helpful. In addition, use can be made of the time of prayer after the formal collects for a more creative approach to intercession. Possibilities include asking different members of the congregation to pray for specific areas of need; having a time of open prayer; writing a litany style of intercessions; and other variations along these lines. The choice of music and the way songs and hymns are introduced also hold possibilities for input helpful to the worship, even when using the traditional format and language.

Despite the new provision some congregations will continue to use the BCP in the 1662 form, which is, of course, still the basic official Prayer Book of the Church of England.

When visiting a church on an occasional basis Readers may find themselves

---

10   The teaching packs issued by PRAXIS, and Grove booklets on the new services, are very helpful for this teaching. Praxis Resources, Sarum College Bookshop, 19 The Close, Salisbury, Wilts SP1 2EE: www.sarum.ac.uk/praxis

12

unfamiliar with the usual local practice. On arriving at the church a question about this will often be met with the response 'Oh! It's just the usual.' Appendix 2 gives a list of questions that may be helpful in tying down just what is meant by 'the usual.'

Readers' own worship needs must be taken into account, especially when they are constantly ministering in a non-eucharistic setting, because of the restraints of their office and the demands of the situation. It is important that they have the opportunity of being able to attend Communion, and to participate on occasions. This is part of a wider need to ensure that Readers have a spiritual home, or base, from which to minister. As with any minister a Reader's spiritual life needs care, so that any subsequent ministry is healthy. The ACORA report has a helpful chapter on spirituality and worship, which covers many of the issues that Readers face in leading worship in rural situations.[12]

Readers can get discouraged if they are given too many ailing services, or services with very small congregations, as their prime sphere of ministry, whilst the incumbent ministers at the more thriving and fuller services. Although many regard such services as important opportunities for ministry, it is nevertheless not healthy or fair for any minister, lay or ordained, to be given the 'crumbs' of ailing services as their staple diet. This matter needs to be addressed both for the sake of individual Readers and their morale, and for the benefit of the congregations and the church as a whole. Two further Grove booklets are useful for those who minister in small congregations,[13] or on Sunday evenings.[14]

ii) Services Outside the Church

Readers are also asked to organize, plan, and lead acts of worship outside the church such as services in centres for the deaf or in hostels or old people's homes; special services for schools, and school assemblies; women's meetings; hospital chapel and ward services; and prison services. These are usually linked with a pastoral ministry with the same group of people, and the building of relationships and trust strengthens the sense of fellowship. This facilitates the worship in what are often difficult conditions in which to minister. For an increasing number of Readers who are in sector ministries this is their prime ministry.

The ecumenical movement has opened up new areas of ministry for Readers. One interesting trend is the increasing number of Readers who are also Methodist Lay Preachers—some operating on their local circuit as a regular preacher. However, more frequent is the involvement of Readers in ecumenical services, as these do not usually involve Communion. Such services offer the opportunity for thinking liturgically and going beyond the restrictions of the usual accepted framework.

---

11 *Common Worship*, p 80.
12 Report of the Archbishops' Commission on Rural Areas (ACORA), *Faith in the Countryside* (Churchman Publishing, 1990) ch 9.
13 David Cutts, *Worship in Small Congregations* (Grove Worship booklet W 108).
14 David Kennedy and David Mann, *Sunday Evening Worship* (Grove Worship booklet W 109).

Ministering at Holy Communion

The present emphasis on the main act of Sunday worship being Communion limits the opportunities for Readers to take full charge of services. However, the readings, intercessions, preaching, distributing of Communion, and limited leading of the service are all open to Readers. Their licence is necessary for regular preaching and also authorizes them to distribute the elements. In practice the role of a Reader varies from as full an involvement as possible, on a par with any ordained member of staff not presiding on that occasion, to an almost entirely passive role with as little as a regular slot on the intercessions rota or an occasional preaching engagement. The role of Readers may include any or all of the following areas. These notes relate to *Common Worship* services of Holy Communion.[15]

Reading: Public reading of God's Word is a valuable ministry when done well. As communicators and ministers of the Word Readers should be able to be an example and role model for others. As well as reading they are often given the responsibility of organizing reading rotas, and ensuring the training of the people in the parish who read the lessons. The reading of lessons, and the intercessions, are both areas where Readers should be ready to encourage the ministry of other lay people, and delegate their own ministry. No 94 in this Grove booklet series looks at the ministry of reading God's word in more depth.[16]

Intercessions: Similarly the leading of people in prayer is a ministry that takes time, careful preparation and is of great value. Readers' world perspectives can be particularly helpful in this role. As with reading they are often given responsibility for the development and organization of intercessory prayer within the parish. The *Common Worship* services encourage a creative approach to leading intercession. No 77 in this Grove booklet series looks at intercessions in worship,[17] and there are also other useful resources.[18]

Leading the Ante-Communion: The opening part of the Communion service can be led by a Reader (as by a deacon). In *Common Worship* this consists of the Gathering and the Liturgy of the Word. In the absolution the 'us' form can be used, and until the Eucharistic Prayer there are no other problems for those who are not ordained. The Notes in *Common Worship* (pp 158–159), explicitly mention the appropriateness of a Reader following the traditional model of a deacon's ministry by bringing in the Gospel, leading the invitation to confession, reading the gospel, preaching the sermon, leading intercessions, preparing the table and the gifts, and taking part in the distribution, the ablutions and the dismissal. A president may delegate any or all parts of the Gathering and the Liturgy of the Word to a

---

15 For an introduction to the Common Worship services of Holy Communion see Mark Beach, *Using Common Worship Holy Communion* (Praxis/Church House Publishing, 2000); Jeremy Fletcher, *Communion in Common Worship: The Shape of Orders One and Two* (Grove Worship booklet W 159); and Colin Buchanan and Charles Read, *The Eucharistic Prayers of Order One* (Grove Worship booklet W 158).
16 Michael Vasey, *Reading the Bible at the Eucharist* (Grove Worship booklet W 94).
17 Michael Vasey, *Intercessions in Worship* (Grove Worship booklet W 77).
18 John Pritchard, *The Intercessions Handbook* (SPCK, 1997); and *Patterns for Worship* (Church House Publishing, 1995).

Reader after the initial greeting, and when no ordained minister is present for this part of the service then a Reader can lead all of it.

In places where the presidency carries much more weight liturgically, the presidency is established by strict adherence to the *Common Worship* rubrics, which reflect the traditional practice. The president gives the initial welcome and greeting, and says the absolution, the collect, the peace and the final blessing, as well as presiding in the eucharistic prayer. In the Communion service the role of Readers is determined not by the pressured necessity of being the sole minister and having to do everything, but by choice. A Reader's role is therefore determined by such questions as: What would it be good to have the Reader do and say in order to show the importance of the whole body of Christ—lay and ordained? To show the whole people of God worshipping together by a giving a visible role to laity? To use the gifts of this particular Reader? To validate the Reader's ministry? and To share the privilege of ministry?

Distributing Communion: Readers usually administer the chalice, but are also authorized to distribute the bread, particularly when a large congregation requires more than one team of ministers for the distribution. When distributing the bread the Reader will need to minister to those not receiving, who come for a blessing. A prayer of blessing can be said—for example, 'May the Lord bless you and keep you. Amen.'

Leading Post-Communion: After the administration the Reader can conclude the service, with or without a (carefully worded!) blessing. This can be done out of choice, but is sometimes necessary for practical reasons, when an ordained minister is on a circuit of services around several churches in a benefice, and needs to leave as soon as is possible.

Distributing Communion to the Sick: According to the Canon, Readers may 'Visit the sick, to read and pray with them…' (E4.2(a)), and they are also permitted 'to distribute the holy sacrament of the Lord's Supper to the people' (E4.2(c)). It is therefore in order for Readers to take Communion to the sick, under the direction of the incumbent. A practical guide to this ministry is offered in another Grove booklet.[19] Such distribution is practised widely for ministry to the sick, both by Communion immediately after a service, and by provision of consecrated elements from a place of safe-keeping (or an aumbry). Both these methods are to be under the direct supervision of the incumbent and are open to other lay people who are licensed by the bishop. However, in some dioceses there is a reluctance to allow this practice at all, and in dioceses where it is allowed in principle, some individual incumbents are reluctant to share the ministry with Readers. Where the ministry is freely shared there is much blessing for all concerned.

Many Readers are asked to take Communion to old people's homes and other institutions where small groups come together for a short service, as well as ministering to individuals. Although a visit by the vicar is particularly appreciated by most parishioners, the lay involvement communicates the care and love of the

---

19   Carolyn Headley, *Home Communion—A Practical Guide* (Grove Worship booklet W 157).

whole church community.

Texts of authorized *Services for Wholeness and Healing*[20] for use with the sick are given in the volume of *Pastoral Services*, authorized as part of the *Common Worship* provision. Shortened Communion services available on card give scope for a short but meaningful service. The rubrics allow for readings and intercessions, and this time can be used for praying for the communicants. This is also an opportunity to pray for others about whom they are concerned, and areas of church and world life. In this way the thoughts of those at home are lifted beyond the confines of their own sickness, and they feel part of the wider community. The prayer which links the elements brought to the home with the service at which they were consecrated is another point of contact with the wider church. Communion is sometimes (but not necessarily) administered in only one kind—the bread.

A taped hymn, or familiar piece of music can be a welcome aid to worship in such contexts. Where facilities allow for tapes to be recorded of the Sunday services, or edited parts, or the sermons, then these may further enrich ministry to those who are housebound.

Practising Extended Communion: The authorized practice outlined above has been more liberally implemented in some dioceses for some time. The shortage of ordained clergy and the desire for regular Communion by rural congregations has led to the regular practice in some areas of Extended Communion for whole communities. The taking of consecrated elements to a small group such as an old people's home is seen as no different in principle from celebrating Communion in one church, and the elements being immediately taken to other churches. To authorise this under certain circumstances (but still seeing it as an exceptional rather than a regular practice), *Public Worship with Extended Communion* has been approved for use from 3 December 2000. It allows for a service to led by a deacon, Reader or other authorized lay person, using bread and wine that has been consecrated elsewhere. The two authorized forms follow Order One and Order Two styles, giving notes for guidance. For communities where geographical isolation makes Communion infrequent, the likelihood is that exceptional need will be deemed as occurring regularly. But diocesan guidelines are likely to vary, with bishops interpreting the agreed policy in different ways.

Readers are trained, able, men and women who will perform this duty responsibly, aware of the privilege of such ministry. In many areas they are also the persons most frequently ministering to a particular community or group, and therefore see this ministry as part of their pastoral care. It is the concern over ecclesiology, with questions about the nature of the church and meaning of ordination, that make some uneasy about this development. This is also one factor behind the call to ordain Readers as OLMs, or at least to ordain more OLMs. However, as argued above, this is to put practical difficulties before an appreciation of the value of a recognized lay ministry. So, for some, the provision for Extended Communion administered by Readers is preferable to ordination for the

---

20 See Colin Buchanan, *Services for Wholeness and Healing* (Grove Worship booklet W 161).

sake of expediency. The whole issue of lay presidency continues to be mentioned, but is not acceptable to many.[21]

An alternative to developing the practice of Extended Communion is to have Communion services less often. Whilst some would like to see this happen as a positive counter-swing to the Parish Communion movement, others would feel that it denied congregations the central act of Christian worship.

Pastoral Offices
i) The Pastoral Context

As already stated there is now a broad understanding of Reader ministry. The pastoral context is not just the setting for preaching, teaching and liturgical ministry but also an integral part of a Reader's calling. Any preaching and teaching ministry which does not reflect something of the pastoral needs of the people, and the community in which they live, is in danger of being over-intellectual and out of touch with those who listen. So the need to be anchored in some way to the pastoral side of parish work is recognized, and the duties outlined in Canon E4 include the pastoral sphere—ministering to the sick, undertaking any pastoral and educational work requested, and taking funerals. In some areas such as the healing ministry and funerals, the pastoral needs directly relate to the liturgical ministry. But in areas where a Reader is not able to officiate, as in baptisms and marriages, they are nevertheless often involved in the preparation and pastoral care of the candidates.

ii) Funeral Ministry

In 1978 Readers were authorized to take funerals, with episcopal permission, and with the goodwill of the family (see Canon E4). Since then there has been a steady increase in their involvement in this ministry and general acceptance by the public of authorized lay ministers taking funeral services. It is now encouraged 'as something to be welcomed in a collaborative context rather than simply as a stop-gap ministry to be performed only in the absence of an available priest,'[22] with a recommendation that the conduct of funerals is included in initial training programmes. The timing of funerals inevitably means that it tends to be Readers who are retired who assist in this way, unless there are exceptional circumstances. For many the taking of services is combined with the pastoral work of visiting the family, and sometimes leads to training as a bereavement counsellor. This is an extremely valuable area of ministry, not only because of the time it takes, but also because some people find a lay person more approachable. It is also a contact point with the community, and with those for whom there is little or no church involvement.

---

21 See Alan Hargrave, *But Who Will Preside?* (Grove Worship booklet W 113) for a review of the issues related to lay presidency.
22 *Moderation of Reader Training 1994-1999*, Archbishops Council, (1999) ¶ 15, p 6.

The new *Common Worship* funeral services will give scope for more choice in the prayers and other content of the service.[23] For a number of years it has been felt that the ASB provision has been very 'thin' and it has been supplemented unofficially by many. Now the resources are significantly increased and include services at the time of death and before and after the funeral itself. This will be helpful in the pastoral care of the bereaved, and will increase the opportunities for Readers in this area of ministry. There are also ideas for the use of symbol and involvement of the family in the funeral service, giving scope for a more meaningful and helpful act of worship.

The question of fees for funeral ministry is dealt with in the Bishops' Regulations. These follow the established principle that as voluntary workers Readers are unable to accept fees, but should be fully reimbursed for expenses and loss of earnings.[24]

iii) Ministry to the Sick

As well as taking Communion to those unable to attend a Eucharist, which is covered above, Readers are often involved in visiting those who are ill. For many this is an important area of their ministry, to which they devote a great deal of time and care. Some Readers have become Lay Chaplains in hospitals, both voluntary and employed by hospital authorities. The *Pastoral Services* of *Common Worship* include a range of services which may be helpful in this context.

iv) Baptisms

Readers are often involved in preparation for baptism. Their role in this could be extended by having some kind of preliminary rite as part of the preparation, and by their presenting the candidates during the baptism service. The idea of staged rites was presented as part of the *On the Way* report but this has not been fully implemented as yet. Some parishes, however, use the brief liturgies offered in the *Emmaus* course for those preparing for Baptism and at other stages in the Christian journey.

The *Common Worship* services of Initiation have several parts of the service where lay ministers and sponsors can participate.[25] Readers' involvement in a service is therefore possible, even if they cannot do the baptism itself.

The desire to be authorized to baptize is very strong among a number of Readers. The identification of particular Readers with particular communities is part of the reason, but there are others. One is the fact that in an emergency any lay person can baptize a person, usually an infant, who may be in danger. As with some of the other emergency provisions the definition of 'emergency' becomes

23 See Trevor Lloyd, *Dying and Death Step by Step* (Grove Worship booklet W 160) and Anne Horton *Using Common Worship Funerals* (Praxis/Church House Publishing, 2000).
24 *Bishops' Regulations for Reader Ministry*, The Archbishops' Council (Church House, January 2000) ¶ 6.4, p 16.
25 See Gilly Myers, *Using Common Worship Initiation* (Praxis/Church House Publishing, 2000); and Colin Buchanan and Michael Vasey, *New Initiation Rites* (Grove Worship booklet W 145).

stretched when resources are pushed to their limit. Consequently the instances when Readers would wish to baptize are increasing. In exceptional circumstances some bishops have given their personal permission for a Reader to baptize, but the House of Bishops as a whole has not approved the practice. Since 1979 the request for permission has been repeatedly put, and the decision against has been repeatedly made. The debate is likely to continue.

Other Contributions to Leading Worship

Individual gifts will lead to other spheres of ministry in worship, which are not 'part and parcel' of the expectation of a Reader, but which can make a great contribution to the life of the church.

As already mentioned, many parishes involve Readers in planning worship either in conjunction with clergy, or as a delegated responsibility. This includes choosing options, and coordinating the participants. They can not only carry such a responsibility themselves, but can also be a resource for training other lay people to share in leading worship.

Where Readers have musical talents then leading worship can have a fuller meaning, in sharing the incumbent's responsibility for choosing hymns, leading a music group, and developing this side of worship. This is of course often delegated to organists and music directors, but there is much to be said for those involved in the ministry of music also having theological knowledge, and being trained as Readers. Where this ministry is delegated then it is beneficial to the worship for clergy, Readers, and organists to work together.

With all such contributions it is not necessary to be a Reader to minister in these ways. The advantage of having Readers lies in their training to think things through at a theological as well as practical level, and being part of the parish leadership to see things in a wider context.

4
Maximizing Potential

Deployment

The demands on Readers, and their availability, varies enormously. In some areas the Readers are virtual 'vicars' to isolated communities, in others they are itinerant and have difficulty bonding with any one worshipping community, in others they are ministering in strong ministry teams which can limit their role drastically, and in others the demands just about match the availability of the Reader(s). There are sometimes concentrations of Readers, both because the parish encourages Reader ministry, and because there is a wealth of gifted men and women who offer themselves. This is often the case in suburban parishes. Releasing this potential should be encouraged, perhaps by allowing a Reader to offer to minister regularly in another parish, or throught the running of a Reader 'pool.'

The ABM Paper on deployment gives very full attention to the matter of using the rich resources that lie in Reader ministry.[26] There are approximately the same number of Readers as there are stipendiary clergy in the Church of England, and many others throughout the Anglican Communion. Being good stewards of this resource is a balance between meeting demand with supply and being mindful of the individual needs of the Reader as a person. The report is aware of the underused resource of Readers and the need of overworked clergy. Where there is reluctance to ask Readers to minister this needs to be addressed. As the paper says:

'It is worth investigating how the supply and demand can be matched, and God's people best served. Whatever may be developed will require:
- A vision of the role of Readers in the overall mission of the Church;
- Flexibility and open-mindedness on the part of diocesan officials;
- Time-consuming care in making arrangements;
- Unselfish generosity and openness on the part of clergy; and
- Unselfish commitment and willingness to go the extra mile on the part of Readers.'[27]

However, it is also necessary to be mindful of the personal needs of Readers and their family. If they are consistently away in itinerant ministry, or on frequent secondment, then attention must be given to where they are receiving their care and nourishment in spiritual terms, where the family has its spiritual 'home,' and to which church family they feel they belong. Support for itinerant ministry is vital.

---

26 ABM Ministry paper No 20, *The Deployment of Readers: A way Forward in Ministry* (November 1998).
27 *ibid*, ¶ 33.

Time Availability

Time availability also varies greatly. Every Reader will have commitments to a greater or lesser extent, whether work or family, or both, and need for personal time, on top of the time given for ministry. Readers who have retired from secular employment will obviously have more time, some are freer through unemployment, and as already mentioned there are some stipendiary Readers in Great Britain. Most Readers, however, are giving of their time on top of other demands. So care needs to be taken in working out realistic time boundaries, which will enable them to have enough time for family, friends, recreation, and personal space.

The conditions for service laid down in the Bishops' Regulations have addressed these issues, calling for a written agreement that takes into account: the particular expression of the individual's ministry; the role of the Reader in the local ministerial team and in relation to the PCC; the arrangements for post-admission training and regular attendance at Reader meetings; the balance between their commitments as Readers and the requirements of their family, work and leisure; the arrangements for reimbursement of expenses incurred through performance of the Reader's duties; and the arrangements for regular meetings between Reader, clergy and other staff. The agreement should be regularly reviewed by the Reader and incumbent together, normally once a year, and at the time of the renewal of licence.[28]

Readers should also keep a record of their ministry, and all the activities they undertake, so that it can be reviewed with the Warden of Readers and discussed with the incumbent.

Clear boundaries, worked out with understanding and agreement, can prevent many problems. Feeling either under-used and therefore under-valued, or over-used and taken for granted, are both common experiences. Sensible, frank discussion at the outset of ministry, plus frequent review (perhaps annually) to adjust to changing circumstances, is helpful to all concerned. This is an area where the voluntary nature of Readership needs to be appreciated. Readers can and should be selective about their involvement.

Support

Being accredited ministers of the church, Readers are answerable to the bishop and he is responsible for them. In practice most dioceses appoint a Warden of Readers, or the equivalent, and many of these have supporting teams or resource groups to help them. Support of Readers can thus be shared at the level of pastoral needs and oversight. However, support for them on a day-to-day basis, encouragement in their ministry, care in appreciating their efforts, and help in areas that need developing, all need to come locally from the staff team. This underlines the need for the incumbent at least occasionally to experience the Reader's ministry.

---

28 *Bishops' Regulations for Reader Ministry*, The Archbishops' Council (Church House, January 2000) ch 5, pp 14–15.

Readers will have to deal with the added opportunity—or stress—of sometimes being a 'go-between,' being both lay people and on the staff team. The opportunity of this situation comes from understanding the value of being close to both the congregation and clergy. In this position there can be constructive two-way feedback through the Reader, for the benefit of the parish. The stress comes from occasions when they are asked to exert their influence, either by the congregation to influence the incumbent, or by the incumbent to influence the congregation. They will be privy to information which opens them up to such pressure. They are also aware of the criticisms and disappointments that abound in parish life, and can feel in a vulnerable position as an 'ear' to all sides. Readers therefore need support, and especially when such pressures are exaggerated in a difficult parish situation. For this reason many Readers now have a person outside the parish to whom they can turn, such as a soul-friend or spiritual director. Incumbents should be aware of the need for these relationships, as it is easy to feel threatened by them. A Reader is a member of the congregation, and as such is within an incumbent's cure of souls, yet a Reader may express a need for additional support.

Some dioceses have implemented pairing systems for support, whereby two Readers meet regularly. This can link an experienced Reader with one who is newly licensed, or just be Readers meeting as colleagues. Deanery groupings of Readers can also give support.

Times of vacancy in the benefice are particularly challenging. There is often heavy reliance on the Reader for liturgical demands and for preaching, arranging worship, and ensuring its smooth running. But the relationships change, and it can be a very unsettling time. The Reader who has had a very close working relationship with the incumbent misses that support and guidance and may be anxious about the future and whether the new incumbent will welcome and use Readers in the parish. In addition the churchwardens' role in relation to the Reader changes considerably, as they assume responsibility for much of what Readers would consider their 'territory.' With the extra demands and uncertainties, relationships can get strained. Much support needs to be given in such a situation, and the Reader must be protected from becoming over-burdened with excessive demands. Similar issues occur when an incumbent is on a period of sabbatical study or extended sick-leave.

The time immediately following an interregnum can also be difficult, especially when the Reader has enjoyed the demands and fulfilment of extra ministry. The new incumbent and wardens need to be aware of the hurt and sense of anti-climax that can be caused for the Reader when the arrival puts a sudden end to valued ministry. This can also be a problem when a new assistant member of staff is appointed.

A Reader coming into a parish, for example after a house move, may find it difficult to be accepted as an ordinary member of a congregation. A helpful general rule is for the Reader to refrain from any ministry for a period of approximately six months, while relationships develop and trust is gained, after which the PCC can make a decision about the Reader being licensed to the parish.

Support not only needs to be pastoral and spiritual but also material. There are many expenses in ministry—travel costs, visual aid materials, books, telephone calls, stationery—to name but a few. Clergy have a well accepted method of reimbursement and expenses claiming procedure. Readers need to have a similarly accepted procedure. Some parishes deal with this monthly as expenses, others give a 'love-gift' annually, or donate the offerings of a particular service to the Readers. Whatever the method, some kind of realistic help must be given to them. It is better when this is formalized, so that it is not seen as a personal matter, with some Readers being able to meet the costs out of their own savings and others needing more reimbursement. A clear and structured method of meeting the financial implications of ministry needs to be agreed with the PCC and incumbent. Those in rural ministry can accumulate vast mileage in their duties, the expense of which needs to be met realistically. Section 6 of the Bishops' Regulations now puts this demand more formally, whilst recognizing the voluntary status of Readers.[29] Readers in training also have substantial costs for books, travel to training sessions, and other expenses.[30] The initial cost of robes is a particularly heavy expense, and help with this is often necessary.

5

Growth Areas for Readers in Liturgy

Looking Back to the Roots

The early history of the office of Reader is interwoven with the history of the minor order of lector, and that of sub-deacon. Throughout the western church these orders had periods of increase in importance over one another and of decline. By the sixteenth century the office of Reader was included in the ordinal of Edward VI, and in 1559 Convocation drew up 'injunctions to be confessed and subscribed by those admitted to the office of Reader.'[31] However, the order declined again and was virtually obsolete by the eighteenth century.

The most significant step towards the office that we now know as Reader was in 1866. The process of identifying a form of recognition for lay ministry had begun about nine years earlier, and the resolution of Convocation in 1866 saw the official revival of the office of Reader, although it was not until 1905 that there were general regulations concerning the ministry. The title Reader has been the official title since 1866. The tendency to refer to Readers as 'Lay Readers' was an

---

29 *ibid*, ch 6, p 16.
30 GS Misc 618, *Reader Ministry and Training, 2000 and Beyond* (2000) ¶ 5.29, p 34.

oddity of usage and habit rather than official policy, although it crept into some official documents.

In 1921 the 1905 regulations were revised and the Readers' Board was formed to exercise oversight. However, that did not see the end of the debate about the recognition of lay ministry. In the 1920s there was discussion about whether the office of sub-deacon ought to be revived, and this debate continued for many years, with a variety of reports being produced. By 1940 both the Houses of the Convocations of Canterbury and York had adopted regulations in respect of Readers, and these included a re-statement of the duties of Readers which are substantially similar to the Canons of today.

In 1969 permission was given for Readers to preach at Holy Communion, and the office also became open to women. In 1978 Readers were allowed to officiate at the burial of the dead, with episcopal permission and the goodwill of the family involved.

The widening of ministry has taken time to evolve, but has been significantly accelerated over the 1980s and 1990s. A Wardens Working Group in 1986 produced a report entitled *The Ministry and Training of Readers in the Church of England*, which challenged and required all dioceses to take a radical look at Reader ministry. For many dioceses the task had already begun and a plethora of new training courses and more dynamic approaches to Reader ministry had been evolving. The 1986 report was an encouragement to continue and bring the training up to an appropriate standard, using more modern and creative education techniques. Training communicators of the faith by methods that fostered good communication skills was part of the vision, but so too was the provision of training that enabled Readers to gain a good theological education and equip them for the range of ministry that many would exercise. A further report by an ACCM working party on theological education, and the setting up of a national moderation process began to work towards ensuring a consistent standard for all Reader training.[32] A National Moderator was appointed in 1990 and dioceses appointed Diocesan Moderators, who were grouped together regionally, to share ideas and information and work toward the development of national standards and methods of training. A Report published in 1994 gives an account of the progress up to that time and highlighted areas that needed to be addressed.[33]

The selection process was also reviewed and a report laid down criteria and guidelines for good practice, helping candidates and the wider church to discern the call to Reader ministry more effectively.[34] Another important document covered principles of good practice in Reader ministry in issuing a new set of Bish-

31 W S Williams, *A History of the Reader Movement in the Church of England* (Parrett and Neves Ltd (CRB), 1932).
32 *The Training of Readers. The Report of the Working Party of the Committee for Theological Education ACCM* (ACCM Occasional Paper No 32, 1989).
33 *The Training of Readers* (ABM Ministry paper No 9, August 1994).
34 *Selection for Reader Ministry: A Report on Criteria and Good Practice*. The Report of a Central Readers' Conference Working Party (ACCM Occasional Paper No 37, 1990).

ops' Regulations.[35] The thirteen-page Appendix by Revd Canon Denys Ruddy entitled 'Reader Ministry in the Parish—Guidelines to Good Practice' was particularly helpful.

Broadening Horizons in the Present

Since the reports of the late 1980s–1990s the work has continued apace, and much progress has been made on raising Reader standards and providing better training, support and working conditions for their ministry. The broadening understanding of the scope of Reader ministry has also continued. The recent round of reports and guidelines[36] have continued to take the ministry forward and keep bishops, and all those involved in Reader ministry, at the task of improving our understanding and practice. A Reader website now makes information more widely accessible—http://www.Readers.cofe.anglican.org

Looking Forward to the Future

Several of the issues facing Readers have already been mentioned: the request for permission for Extended Communion to be practised more freely; the request to be allowed to baptize; and the hope that the office will remain a broadly defined recognition of lay-ministry, as being a calling that is complementary to the existing ministries.

But there is excitement too, with new opportunities for dynamic and creative liturgy and mission-oriented services in *Common Worship*, involvement in *Alpha* and *Emmaus* courses, and growth in acceptance of lay ministry and shared ministry. I would also hope that the increasing awareness of the office by incumbents and the church as a whole would continue and that there would be a further increase in the number of young candidates and those from ethnic minorities.

What still needs addressing is the relationship of Readers to OLM and NSM ordained clergy, especially those committed to a permanent diaconate, and the issue of whether many Readers may, in fact, be called to be ordained as OLMs. But along with this is the need to find good and appropriate ways of recognizing lay ministry and valuing it for its distinctive contribution. The profusion of local schemes for authorizing a whole spectrum of ministries shows that there is a stirring for this to done. What is missing at present is any church-wide definition that works at local level. Part of this dilemma is the underlying concern that ordination itself has been insufficiently clarified in the number of variations that have sprung up.

---

35 *Report on Bishops' Regulations for Reader Ministry. The Report of a Central Readers' Conference Working Party* (ACCM Occasional Paper No 36, 1990).

36 *Selection for Reader Ministry* (ABM Policy Paper No 7, January 1998); *The Deployment of Readers: A Way Forward in Ministry* (ABM Ministry paper No 20, November 1998); *Moderation of Reader Training 1994–1999*, Archbishops Council (1999); *Bishops' Regulations for Reader Ministry*, The Archbishops' Council (Church House, January 2000); GS Misc 618, *Reader Ministry and Training, 2000 and Beyond*, Ministry Division (September 2000).

6
Reader Training in Worship and Liturgy

The training that Readers receive undergirds their God-given gifts with greater knowledge and improved communication skills. Well-trained Readers can renew the traditional ministry, and strengthen the renewed ministry, of the church and encourage the ministry of all believers.

Initial Training Programmes

The revolution in the provision of initial training of Readers that began in the late 1980s and early 1990s, outlined above, has produced some excellent training schemes. The National Moderator (first appointed in 1990), and the Reader Training Panel (formed in 1999), now oversee the training of Readers. The Training Panel is chaired by a member of the Theological Education and Training Committee of the Ministry Division of the Archbishops' Council, tying Reader training into that of the wider church ministry more closely. Part of the moderation process involves a quinquennial moderation of all schemes with interim annual reviews, making the oversight and support of the training quite significant. The recommendations made in 1999 form the current agenda for those involved in Reader training and the comprehensive report of September 2000 builds on this, giving careful attention to all areas of initial and continuing Reader training.

The tutorial and essay system, which had been in place for many years, has been replaced by courses that involve a variety of education methods, working towards The Church of England Reader's Certificate. For isolated candidates, those stationed abroad in the forces and those with special training needs, individual courses may still be necessary. Extension studies programmes, distance learning schemes, and the Open Theological College, have also been used for individual candidates who are unable to join group schemes. But the general shift is towards training with others, working in groups, integrating Reader training with other kinds of ministry training, and making the approach much more practically and experientially orientated.

There is an increasing move towards using schemes that recognize past ministry, and give credit for existing academic and experiential knowledge. This is sometimes linked with vocational education using colleges or courses, and can be part of a system of credits and modules that build towards an accredited qualification or certificate. Some dioceses are also committed to the principle of lifelong learning and see the initial Reader training as only one part of a continuing process of learning, which began before the training period and will go on all through the Reader's ministry. Some schemes include the practical aspects of ministry within the syllabus, with an assessment of competences in areas of ministry, alongside the more usual approach to learning.

With regard to worship this means that initial training needs to include both the historical and theological ground on which our liturgy is founded, and also practical sessions. Some of the common threads in the area of worship and liturgy are as follows:[37]

Preaching: Training includes the theory of preaching; its aims and goals; techniques; practical sessions on voice production, presentation, and methods of preparing; video recording and playback for working on style. In addition all other parts of the training can have assessment methods which ensure that what is learned can be communicated—*eg* with sermons, presentations, and talks. The difference between teaching and preaching can also be addressed, with sessions on how people learn and methods of teaching—not necessarily for use during services, but for all types of teaching situations. The report on training specifically calls for instruction on preaching skills in the handling of biblical passages appropriately and imaginatively; setting Bible passages and stories in their wider context; using commentaries and other tools; the craft of sermon construction; preaching at a range of services to different congregations; addressing a range of ethical issues in formal and informal settings; evangelistic preaching; and effective delivery, including the use of sound systems.

Worship: Learning about worship entails understanding the nature of worship and place of liturgy; the place of worship in daily life and in the world; the liturgical history of the church, and the roots of our current liturgy; current developments and future possibilities; examination of non-verbal liturgy, and exploration of its potential. Practical aspects particularly noted in the report on training are conducting morning and evening prayer; reading the Bible in church; leading intercessions; leading the ministry of the word in Communion; assisting at the administration of consecrated bread and wine; contributing to the planning of worship; devising and leading a variety of services such as all age worship; and assisting at baptism and conducting funeral services and interments (although these may be left to post-licensing training).

In all training, whether in worship or other subjects, the role of the Reader in the world as well as in the church needs to be stressed and developed. Readers are not in training to be clerics, but to be a world/church link in all worship, preaching, and living. So as well as training to take opportunities open in the church, there should be equal emphasis on training to take the opportunities that lie open in the world, the family, and the community.

Readers' training needs to help them develop their own worship of God. It is all too easy when licensed to switch from being 'in the pew' to being 'up-front,' and to see that as an irreversible change. Consequently one's own worship can suffer. There needs to be emphasis on the importance of still worshipping 'in the pew,' being with the congregation, being alongside, and sharing in the worship. It is a great sadness to come across Readers who only go to church when they are to be involved in the service, and who take the attitude that 'I don't need to go this morning, because I'm not doing anything.'

---

37 See GS Misc 618, *Reader Ministry and Training* ¶ 5.13–5.15, pp 28–29.

In-service Training

For Readers to maintain their integrity as preachers and leaders of worship, continuing education is important. The expectation of continuing education is reflected in the Bishops' Regulations as one aspect of the written agreement in the conditions of service,[38] and in the reports on Training.[39] In the latter it is also hoped that CME (continuing ministerial education) will be well supported financially and in the quality of what is provided. The usefulness of joint CME for Readers with clergy and others who minister, is being addressed in some areas. The commitment to collaborative ministry makes it helpful to see Readers as an important part of the ministry team of a whole diocese, not just a parish. Joint ventures in CME also have other benefits in terms of building relationships, facilitating wider deployment as a consequence, and creating a more stimulating learning environment as those with different approaches discuss and learn from one another.

There are some funds available centrally to help in supporting further learning. Where a Reader would like to enter into a specific area of study, and has the support of the Warden of Readers for their project and their application, a small grant can be made by the CRC from the Adams Fund, which exists for educational purposes.

In terms of worship, CME is vital at this time of change. To be in the forefront of liturgical thinking there must be a willingness to keep abreast of liturgical developments. This should involve keeping up to date with publications from the Liturgical Commission and General Synod, attending study days and conferences, and being prepared to implement what is learned. Solely maintaining the traditional forms of worship, without openness to developments, can stifle growth, and can earn Readers a bad reputation. Change is not always necessary and the right thing for a given situation, but unwillingness to even consider the possibilities encourages a fossilizing of worship. The end of authorization of the ASB will demand new approaches.

Another area that has been addressed by the CRC and Bishops' Regulations is the need for continuing review of a Reader's ministry, as with ordained ministry. If the high ideals of Reader ministry are to be maintained, then a method of review, appraisal, and opportunities for developing and learning, is important. Combining the re-licensing programme of a diocese with some such appraisal is practised by most dioceses, and is stated as a requirement in the new Bishops' Regulations and training report.[40] This can only happen when there is a real option to re-license, and this presupposes that it must be possible to withhold a licence. Such a system is obviously very unpopular and hurtful, but if Readership is to be seen as a role-model or 'flag-ship' for lay ministry, then it must be of the highest possible standard. Review also opens up possibilities for encouragement

---

38 *Bishops' Regulations for Reader Ministry*, The Archbishops' Council (Church House, January 2000) ¶ 5.2, p 14.
39 *Moderation of Reader Training 1994–1999*, Archbishops Council (1999) ¶ 16, p 6; and GS Misc 618, *Reader Ministry and Training, 2000 and Beyond* (Ministry Division, 2000) ¶6, pp 39–44.
40 *op cit*, ¶ 5.4, p 14; and *ibid* ¶ 6.12–6.13, p 43.

to develop ministry, and possibly to specialize in a particular area—for which further training may be appropriate. In some areas this is again linked into accredited modules which build towards further academic goals.

Some kind of appraisal is also desirable because of the fact that so many Readers minister in isolation. They are often ministering in the absence of the incumbent, and therefore are rarely observed in action by the one responsible for them. Involvement of those who receive their ministry could therefore be a helpful part of any appraisal system both for encouragement and to highlight areas of need. Appraisal should have a constructive and positive role in affirming and strengthening a Reader, and helping to develop ministry.

A difficult area related to appraisal and re-licensing is the retirement of Readers from ministry. Over the age of 70 most dioceses operate an annual Permission To Officiate (PTO). Many Readers over 70 still have much to give in ministry. For others the ability to minister is waning, which some of them will recognize for themselves and others will be unable to come to terms with. The withholding of the PTO then becomes difficult, and the decision of whether or not to allow ministry to continue is taken on pastoral grounds. There can of course be no hard and fast rules concerning this, but for the sake of Reader ministry as a whole, and for the specific congregations, courageous decisions sometimes need to be taken.

The title of Reader Emeritus has been used as a way of keeping a link with Reader ministry, although retired from active duties. Retired Readers can be invited to Reader events and do not need to feel cast aside. The title Emeritus suggests the office of Reader is continuing and that therefore there is a continuing Permission To Officiate. It needs to be clarified in dioceses where this title is used, as to whether a formal annual PTO is required to minister, or whether perpetual permission is given by this title, or whether it is being given to honour the past work and service of the Reader .

7
Conclusion

If the lay ministry of the church, that emerges from the congregations, and is gifted and called by God is not released, the church will suffer greatly. If that ministry is not trained then there is a danger of reverting to a clergy/lay divide, because of a lack of confidence in lay ministry. A trained accredited lay ministry, which aims at high standards and thereby becomes a complimentary ministry to that of the ordained clergy, is of immense value, in its own right and as a catalyst to release and enable other lay ministry in the parishes. A suitable conclusion is provided by the ABM Paper on Deployment of Readers:

'Gradually the church is moving away from the concept of Readers "helping" the clergy in their ministry to a recognition that Readers exercise a God-given ministry as trained lay pastors, preachers, teachers and leaders, working along-side other ministers, lay and ordained. As such, they are uniquely placed among neighbours and colleagues, friends and family, to proclaim the love of God as revealed in Jesus Christ for our salvation.'

Appendix 1
Canons Relating to Readers

Canon E4 States (October 2000 edition):

1   A lay person, whether man or woman, who is baptized and confirmed and who satisfies the bishop that he is a regular communicant of the Church of England may be admitted by the bishop of the diocese to the office of Reader in the Church and licensed by him to perform the duties which may lawfully be performed by a Reader according to the provisions of paragraph 2 of this Canon or which may from time to time be so determined by Act of Synod.

2   It shall be lawful for a Reader:
   (a) to visit the sick, to read and pray with them, to teach in Sunday school and elsewhere, and generally to undertake such pastoral and educational work and to give such assistance to any minister as the bishop may direct;
   (b) during the time of divine service to read Morning and Evening Prayer (save for the Absolution), to publish banns of marriage at Morning or Evening Prayer (on occasions on which a layman is permitted by the statute law so to do, and in accordance with the requirements of that law), to read the Word of God, to preach, to catechize the children, and to receive and present the offerings of the people;
   (c) to distribute the holy sacrament of the Lord's Supper to the people.

2A The Bishop may also authorize a Reader to bury the dead or read the burial service before, at or after a cremation but only, in each case, with the goodwill of the persons responsible and at the invitation of the minister of a parish or an extra-parochial place within the meaning of section 1 of the Deaconesses and Lay Ministry Measure 1972.
   When a cure is vacant the reference in this paragraph to the minister of a parish shall be construed as a reference to the rural dean.

3   The bishop of every diocese shall keep a register book wherein shall be entered the names of every person whom he has either admitted to the office of Reader or licensed to exercise that office in any place.'

The current Canons contain measures relating to Readers not only in E4, but also in:
   E5—relating to the nomination and admission of Readers.
   E6—relating to the licensing of Readers.
   B43—The Ecumenical Relations Measure of 1988 refers to the duties Readers may perform as part of ecumenical projects—Canon B43 (in paragraph 6) enables Readers to perform duties similar to those they are authorized to perform in the Church of England. This is providing they have the approval of the local incumbent. If ministry is on a regular basis then the bishop's permission is also required.
   B44—sets out in detail how Readers can function in an LEP.

Appendix 2
Check-list, When Asked for 'Just the Usual, Please!'

As it is a courtesy to respect local custom, the visiting Reader will need to be aware of usual practice. However, most congregations are grateful to visiting officiants and understand if not everything is done exactly as they expect!

Prior to Preparing the Service

Which form of service is to be used: *Common Worship*, contemporary or traditional, or the BCP unaltered? Which options are used in the order of service, from alternatives within the text (*eg* which Lord's Prayer?), and as allowed from resources in *CW* (*eg* which confession and absolution), or as referred to in the rubrics in BCP (*eg* which canticles?). How many hymns are there, and at what points in the service? Who chooses the hymns, and if the Reader, who should be notified of the choice and by when? Which lectionary is being used (*CW* or BCP)? Which Track is being followed (when applicable)? Does a particular reading need to be the focus for preaching (*eg* if preaching through a biblical book)? Who is reading the lessons, and are there pew Bibles for which page numbers need to be given? Who is leading the prayers of intercession, and if the Reader who can give names of locally sick people and local situations that require prayer? Are robes normally worn? What time will the church be open and who will prepare the church for the service?

Before the Service

Normal procedure for coming in and going out including: Is there a choir? Does the choir process? Is there a vestry prayer before and/or after the service? How does the service end? Does the Reader go to the vestry or to the church door if there is not a vestry prayer? Which route does the procession/minister take? Is it usual to bow, genuflect, pause, or walk straight to the seat? Where is the Reader to be seated? Is the service conducted from there or from the lectern?

Are the Creed, Lord's Prayer, Collects, Responses etc said or sung? (and if sung—what chant, and is a note given?) Does the choir and minister turn to the cross/altar for the Creed? Does the music just start or are hymns normally announced? Is the psalm sung or said? If said then is this antiphonally or together, sitting or standing? How are prayers normally introduced *eg* repeat first line, congregation join in automatically, or invite congregation to say together...? Do the congregation sit, kneel, or stand to pray, and do they need to be told to do so? Is it usual practice to preach from the pulpit, the body of the church, or the lectern?

How is the collection/offertory presented, and what is the usual way of receiving it? *ie* Where is it received—at the altar or the chancel steps, and is prayer silent during the hymn or a public prayer after the hymn?

At what point are notices given out? Is there a list of local notices? Are there any Banns of Marriage to be read? (A Reader is authorized to read Banns of Marriage, and to sign the Banns register, but not a Banns certificate).